The At-Home Olympics

Michael Wagner
Illustrated by Bettina Guthridge

CELEBRATION PRESS

Pearson Learning Group

When Dad moved into his new apartment, there wasn't much room to play. If we were going to have any fun at all, we needed some games for small areas. I made up a few.

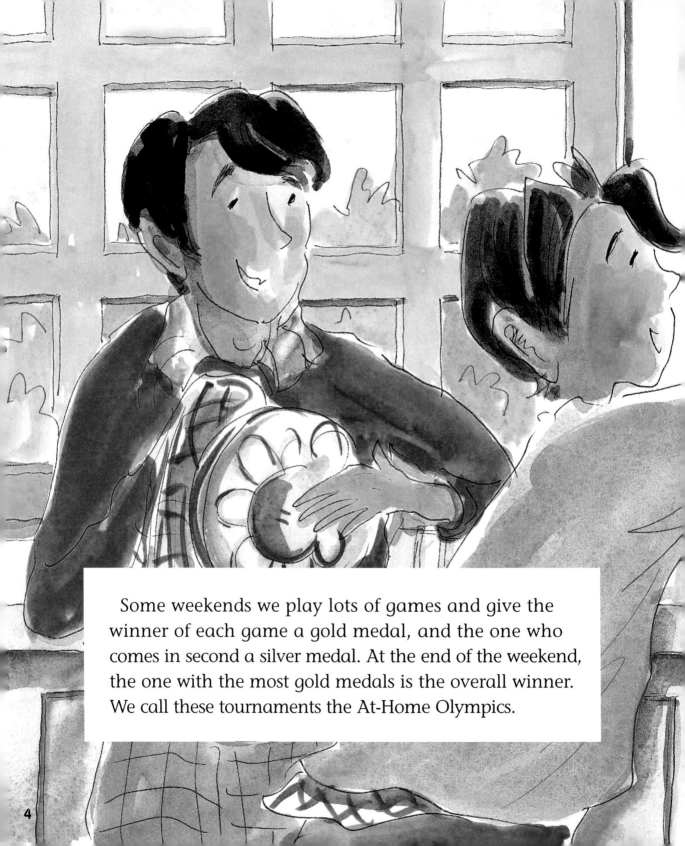

Some weekends we play lots of games and give the winner of each game a gold medal, and the one who comes in second a silver medal. At the end of the weekend, the one with the most gold medals is the overall winner. We call these tournaments the At-Home Olympics.

Saturday

1 P.M. Ping Pong Hand Tennis

4 P.M. Hallway Soccer

Sunday

10 A.M. Mixed-Ball Bowling

1 P.M. Four-Room Marathon

Last weekend we played four made-up games. I worked out which ones. To keep it fair, I chose two games I was good at and two games Dad was good at.

In the history of the At-Home Olympics, Dad has won five tournaments, and the other four were ties. If I could win one of my weaker events, I would have a chance to be the overall winner for the first time.

I organized it so there was time to rest between events, and so we'd finish before Helen, Dad's new girlfriend, arrived at 5 o'clock on Sunday.

Gold Silver

Dad

qson

7

Event 1: Ping Pong Hand Tennis

1st set:	21-11
2nd set:	21-8
3rd set:	18-21
4th set:	3-21
5th set:	

I decided to start with Ping Pong Hand Tennis because I was the favorite, and I wanted an early win. We play this game on the kitchen table. We use framed photographs for a net, and coasters for paddles, one in each hand. I'm good with both hands. That's why I'm the favorite.

I beat Dad in the first two sets, 21–11 and 21–8, but then I made the mistake of relaxing. That let Dad back in the game. He won the next two sets 21–18 and (I couldn't believe it!) 21–3.

Gold   Silver

Dad
Jason

Event 1: Ping Pong Hand Tennis
1st set: 21–11
2nd set: 21–8
3rd set: 18–21
4th set: 3–21
5th set:

It all came down to the fifth set, and my form was
bad. I needed to work harder.

When it got to 19–all, I said to Dad, "Normally
you fall apart about now."

"Just serve the ball," said Dad.

So I did. I served it to his left hand, normally a certain point for me, but Dad twisted his right hand around and lobbed the ball back. I smashed it back at him. His return nicked the top of a photo frame and bobbled onto my side of the table. I dove forward but could not reach it. The score was 20–19—match point to Dad.

I served to his left hand again. He twisted around and got it back. I whacked it across the table. He reached down, almost to the floor, and scooped it back into play. It lobbed up for another smash. This was going to be the leveler. I jumped up and smacked it onto Dad's side. He blocked it. It came back fast. I could only lob it up. I stepped back, ready for Dad to smash it, but Dad was clever—he just tipped it over the photo frames. I was too far back to reach it. He won, three-sets-to-two, 21–19 in the fifth set!

My plan to take an early lead was ruined.

RIGHT
WAY UP

   The rubber ball we use for Hallway Soccer weighs
almost nothing, so it doesn't hurt even if it hits you
hard. We put cardboard boxes at each end of the
corridor—they're the goals. The hardest part is just
getting the ball past the other player. You have to either
bounce it off the walls, get it between their legs, or try to
bend it around them. If my legs were as big as Dad's we
would be even, but they're not, so he was the favorite.
I really needed a win.

   For the whole first quarter, we just kept kicking the ball
into each other's legs.

	Gold	Silver
Dad	1	
Jason		1

Event 2:
Hallway Soccer

Half time: zero–all

RIGHT WAY UP

At half time it was zero–all.

Eight minutes into the third quarter, I charged up to Dad's end of the hallway and slammed the ball at his goals. Dad stuck a leg out. The ball bounced back so hard it shot between my legs and rolled all the way to the goals at my end. Dad scored!

"Lucky break, Dad," I said.

"There's no such thing as luck in sports," said Dad.

"Yeah, right."

Gold
Dad   1
Jason

Event 2: Hallway Socc
Half time: zero-all
Three-quarter time: 1-
Final quarter:

At the third quarter Dad led 1–zero. Things were looking bad.

Thirty seconds into the final quarter, we were locked in battle in the middle of the hallway when Dad suddenly stumbled. He leaned on the side wall to get his balance back, leaving half the hallway open for a split second. I slotted the ball past him, and it bounced into the goals. 1–all. It wasn't over yet!

For the next fourteen minutes, Dad did nothing but block his goals. I must have kicked the ball into him fifty times.

"Thirty seconds and it's all over," said Dad, when he had a moment to look at his watch.

"That's all I need," I said. But I was worried. I didn't know how to get past him. Then it came to me.

With the ball at my feet, I stared at the right wall near Dad's knee. He leaned across to block the kick. But when I kicked it, I flicked it over his shoulder instead. I caught him going the wrong way. The ball sailed past his head and dropped into the goals. 2–1. The alarm on Dad's watch went off. Game over! I had won! I could still win the At-Home Olympics!

Mixed-Ball Bowling requires lots of patience—that's why I'm the favorite and not Dad. We get four balls each: a squash ball, a golf ball, a tennis ball, and a rubber band ball. We roll them toward a target marble.

When we've bowled all our balls, the closest one to the target marble gets a point. If you've got the two closest balls, you get two points. You can get up to four points in one game. We agreed to play fourteen games. After that, the one with the highest score wins.

	Gold	Silver
Dad	1	1
Jason	1	1

Event 3: Mixed-Ball Bowling

After 14 games: 11-all

We started in the hallway, but played right through the apartment—even down the step between the kitchen and the living room.

I won a point on the first game and another on the second, but Dad picked up three points on the third. After fourteen games the score was 11–all. That meant we had to keep playing until someone had a clear two-point lead.

An hour later, during the twenty-second game, the score was 15-all, but I had been playing badly. The first three of my balls had gone way past the marble. Dad had the three closest balls—and two of them were blocking the target. His fourth ball went way off to the left, so it was no problem.

I had only one ball to stop him from taking a three-point lead, and the game! As I picked up the rubber-band ball, I had no choice. I had to knock all of Dad's balls out of the way.

I rolled the ball hard at the two blocking balls. It headed straight for them, but then it started bouncing. It bounced right over Dad's balls. "Oh no!" I thought. Then it did something unexpected. It crashed into the marble, knocking it back to the wall . . . where my first three balls were sitting!

I had missed the blocking balls, but scored three points anyway! Suddenly, I was leading with two gold medals.

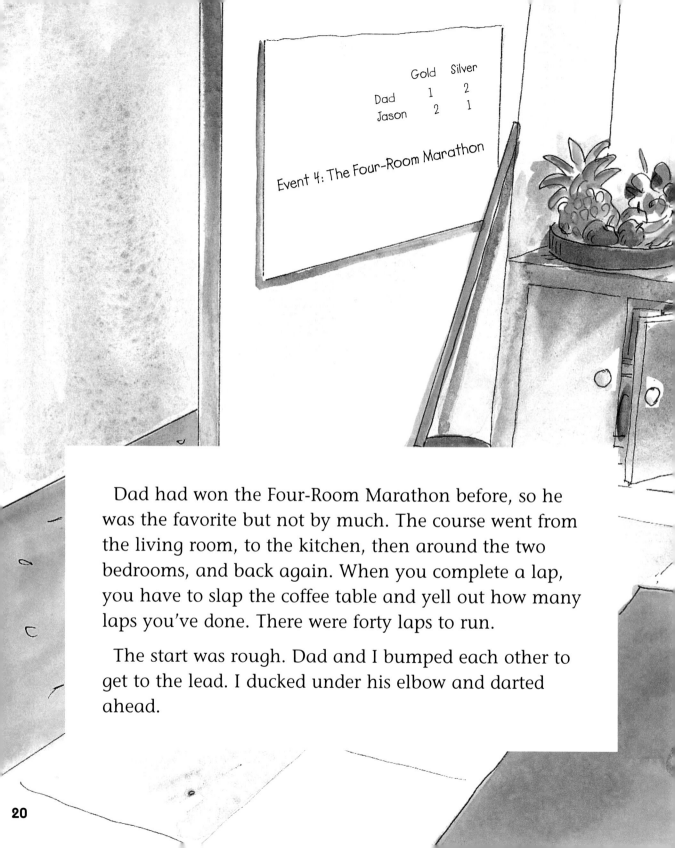

	Gold	Silver
Dad	1	2
Jason	2	1

Event 4: The Four-Room Marathon

Dad had won the Four-Room Marathon before, so he was the favorite but not by much. The course went from the living room, to the kitchen, then around the two bedrooms, and back again. When you complete a lap, you have to slap the coffee table and yell out how many laps you've done. There were forty laps to run.

The start was rough. Dad and I bumped each other to get to the lead. I ducked under his elbow and darted ahead.

I led for the first twelve laps, but Dad was never far behind. As I slapped the coffee table and yelled, "Twelve!" Dad slapped it as well and dashed past me. I didn't even know he was there!

For the next nine laps I couldn't get past him. He kept blocking me. Then in the twenty-second lap, Dad stumbled as he jumped up the step. I raced past him.

"Hey . . ." said Dad, but I was gone!

   When the fortieth lap began, Dad was breathing down my neck. I darted out of the living room and through the kitchen. He was right there. I ran through his bedroom and up the corridor into mine. I couldn't shake him. I threw myself across the bed and back into the corridor. He was gaining on me. I dove from the living room doorway to the coffee table. We landed at the same time. And he was right beside me! I slapped it and yelled, "Forty!" I was only a split second slower than Dad! His height helped him in that final lunge.

I was devastated. My big chance to win the At-Home Olympics had slipped through my fingers.

"I can't take another tie," I said. "We need another race."

"I agree," said Dad, "but there's not enough time." Helen was going to arrive in half an hour.

"We'll make it something quick," I said.

"Like what?" said Dad.

"A thumb-wrestle," I said. "It'll be over in minutes."

"Okay," said Dad, and we locked hands.

What you have to do in a thumb-wrestle is hold the other person's thumb down for a count of three.

We wrestled for thirty straight minutes, without a break! My fingers were numb. Dad's hand was dripping with sweat.

I heard the doorbell. "That was the door, Dad," I said, not relaxing my grip.

"No tricks," said Dad. "Just play the game."

"But Dad," I said.

Dad refused to listen. Then there was a loud bang on the door. Dad got scared—and that was all I needed. I pinned his thumb and said, "One!"

"What?" said Dad.

"Two!" I said.

"Hey!" said Dad, realizing what was going on.

"Three!" I yelled.

I let go of his hand and danced around the room with my arms in the air. I had won! The At-Home Olympics were finally mine!

A few minutes later, Helen flicked on the CD player. It pumped out the national anthem. I stepped onto a chair and stood to attention. I was so proud, I had tears in my eyes.

"You were good, Dad," I muttered, "but I was better."

"There's always next time, Jason," whispered Dad, still standing to attention. "There's always next time."

	Gold	Silver
Dad	2	3
Jason	3	2